That's So Funny
I Forgot to Laugh!

■ ■ ■ ■ ■ ■ ■ ■ ■ ■ ■ ■ ■

Jokes, Jokes, and More Jokes

ALLEN COHEN

A TRUMPET CLUB ORIGINAL BOOK

Published by
Dell Publishing
a division of
Bantam Doubleday Dell Publishing Group, Inc.
666 Fifth Avenue
New York, New York 10103

Dell ® TM 681510, Dell Publishing Co., Inc.

ISBN: 0-440-84300-6

Printed in the United States of America

September 1987

10 9 8 7 6

WFH

For Adam and Zachary,
who I hope will like this book
when they're old enough to read it.

Thanks to
Judy, Diana, Harold, Myrna, Milton, Louise, Alan,
Julie, Barry, Sue, Jeff, Ellen, Ken, Denise, Rob,
Michael, and most of all, to Leslie.

The History of Jokes
A Very Brief Survey

Jokes have been around as long as people have. Cavemen used to sit around their campfires at night, telling knock-knock jokes. Back then, though, instead of saying "Knock, knock," they would knock each other on the head with their clubs.

Emperors and kings have always known the power of laughter. For instance, Napoléon used to tell jokes as he conquered Europe. And everyone always laughed (or else).

Then there was Thomas Edison, the great inventor. After many years, he invented the light bulb. Two days later, he invented the light-bulb joke.

Even Albert Einstein loved a good joke. But sometimes the laugh was on him, especially when he tried to play the violin. Once when he had trouble keeping up with the other musicians, one of them turned to him and said, "What's the matter, Einstein, can't you count?"

So it looks like jokes will go on as long as people do. In times to come, maybe you will contribute your own, and as mankind advances into the future it may be your mission to explore strange new jokes, to seek out new lines and new situations, to boldly joke where no one has joked before!

What's a Mexican weather report?

Chili today, hot tamale.

■

**Why are Saturday and Sunday
stronger than the other days?**

Because the others are weakdays.

■

When are farmers mean?

When they pull the ears off corn.

■

When are cooks mean?

When they beat eggs and whip cream.

■

When are hoboes mean?

When they hit the road.

■

When is a miner mean?

When he strikes gold.

■

When are politicians mean?

When they beat around the bush.

**When the Indians in the movies
sneak up on the cowboys,
why don't the cowboys
ever hear them?**

Because they walk on tepee-toes.

Where does Batman take a shower?

In the Bat-room.

■

How many letters are there in the alphabet during Christmastime?

Twenty-five: Noel (no L)!

■

What do you get when you cross a trumpet with an apple?

Tooty-fruity.

■

What's the quickest way to double your money?

Fold it in half.

■

Why do melons have to have a formal wedding?

Because melons just canteloupe (can't elope).

■

What's the difference between a piano and a fish?

You can tune a piano, but you can't tuna fish.

Why do baseball fields last longer than football fields?

Because diamonds are forever.

■

What did Delaware?

I don't know, Alaska.

■

Where's the largest pencil in America?

Pennsylvania.

■

Who is buried in Grant's Tomb?

(You can answer this one yourself!)

Here's a tricky riddle that's hundreds of years old:

As I was going to St. Ives
I met a man with forty wives
Every wife had forty sacks
Every sack had forty cats
Every cat had forty kits (kittens).
Kits, cats, sacks, and wives,
How many were going to St. Ives?

(The answer is **one**. All those others were going the other way!)

SMALL TALK
WITH
JIM AND
KIM

JIM: Did you hear the one about the three holes in the ground?

KIM: No.

JIM: Well, well, well.

KIM: Did you hear the one about the roof?

JIM: No.

KIM: It's over your head.

JIM: Did you hear the one about the cave?

KIM: No.

JIM: It's too deep for you.

KIM: Pete and Repeat were in a boat. Pete fell out. Who was left?

JIM: Repeat.

KIM: Pete and Repeat were in a boat. . . .

JIM: I ripped my shirt and my mom tried to fix it.

KIM: How'd she do?

JIM: Sew-sew.

KIM: Look, here are some smart pills. If you eat them you get smarter. Try a couple.

JIM: Ugh! These aren't pills, they're lima beans!

KIM: See, you're getting smarter already!

JIM: What has whiskers and a tail, washes it-self with its tongue, catches mice, and barks like a dog?

KIM: I have no idea.

JIM: A cat.

KIM: But you said it barks like a dog!

JIM: I didn't want to make it too easy for you.

KIM: Did you hear about the lady whose left arm and leg were eaten by a shark?

JIM: No.

KIM: Well, she's all right now.

JIM: Where we used to live we had lots of snow, and we'd run around and play in the snow all day.

KIM: That's nothing. Where we used to live, we had snoo.

JIM: Snoo? What's snoo?

KIM: I don't know, what's snoo with you?

MOTHER: Jim, you shouldn't be watching TV. You were supposed to do your homework after you did the dishes.

JIM: It's okay, Mom—I haven't done the dishes yet.

JIM: Why do elephants paint their toenails red?

KIM: I don't know.

JIM: So when they hide in the trees, they'll look like cherries.

KIM: But nobody's ever seen an elephant in a tree!

JIM: See, it works!

MOTHER: I'm going to the drugstore to buy some toiletries.

JIM: Don't be silly, Mom. Toilets don't grow on trees!

KIM: Doctor, last night I dreamed I was a te-pee. Then I had another dream where I was a wigwam! What's wrong with me?

DOCTOR: You need to relax; you're two tents.

FIRST CANNIBAL: I don't like my mother-in-law.

SECOND CANNIBAL: Then just eat the vegetables.

WAITER: What'll you have?

KIM: Make me a sundae.

WAITER: *Poof.* You're a sundae.

KIM: No, really, I want a sundae.

WAITER: Sorry, we're out of sundaes, but I can make you one Monday!

JIM: You're making the whole beach crazy.
KIM: I am not!
JIM: Well, I saw you drive a dune buggy.

KIM: How do you know that Sue's house is a Japanese restaurant?
JIM: When I see Sue, she's (sushi's) there.

KIM: What time is it?
JIM: Ten to.
KIM: Ten to what?
JIM: Ten to your own business!

JIM: Would you call me a cab?
KIM: Okay, you're a cab.

JIM: How can I get rid of excess weight?
KIM: Try cutting off your head!

JIM: Why don't you make like a tree and leaf?
KIM: Well, why don't you make like a banana and split?

EVE: Adam, do you love me?
ADAM: Who else?

THE FRUIT
AND
VEGETABLE
HALL OF
FAME

What sings and is nuts?
Donny and Marie Almond.

■

What's green and tap-dances?
Bean Kelly.

■

What else is green and tap-dances?
Fred Asparagus.

■

What's hot and goes with Fred Asparagus?
Ginger Radish.

■

What's green and sings "Love me Tender"?
Elvis Parsley.

■

What's green and champion of the world?
The Italian Scallion.

What's purple and swings through the jungle?

Tarzan of the Grapes.

What's orange, lives in New Jersey, and sings?

Juice Springsteen.

·

What eats honey and grows on trees?

Yogi Pear.

·

What has a Mohawk haircut and comes in bags?

Mr. Tea.

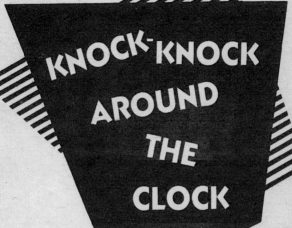

KNOCK-KNOCK AROUND THE CLOCK

Knock, knock.
Who's there?
Howard.
Howard who?
Howard you like to hear another knock-knock joke?

Knock, knock.
Who's there?
Little old lady.
Little old lady who?
I didn't know you could yodel!

Knock, knock.
Who's there?
Gorilla.
Gorilla who?
Gorilla me a hamburger.

■

Knock, knock.
Who's there?
Amos.
Amos who?
Amosquito just bit me!

■

Knock, knock.
Who's there?
Andy.
Andy who?
Andy just bit me again!

Knock, knock.
Who's there?
Banana.
Banana who?
Banana banana. Knock, knock.
Who's there?
Banana banana.
Banana banana who?
Banana banana banana. Knock, knock.
Who's there?
Orange.
Orange who?
Orange you glad I didn't say banana again?

ANIMAL RIDDLES, OR LIFE-STYLES OF THE RANCH AND FARMYARD

What's worse than finding a worm in an apple?

Finding half a worm.

■

Where do sheep get their hair cut?

At the baa-baa shop.

■

Where are guinea pigs from?

Hamsterdam.

■

Who builds houses for snakes?

A boa contractor.

■

What do you call a tedious snake?

A bore constrictor.

■

What kind of snake does a great job on windows?

A window viper.

What do you call a cat that eats pickles?

A sour puss.

Why is the king of the jungle the laziest animal?

He's always lion around.

■

How do you stop a bull from charging?

Take away its credit cards.

■

What do you call a sleepy bull?

A bull dozer.

■

What do you call it when two ducks collide in midair?

A quack-up.

■

How can you help out a family of poor ducks?

Pay their bills.

■

What do you get when you cross a bee with a cow?

A humburger.

Why does a frog make a good outfielder?

He's great at catching flies.

■

Why did the rabbits go on strike?

They wanted a raise in celery.

■

Why did the dog go "Birch! Birch!"?

Because it was the only bark he knew.

■

What's purple, squirts ink, and knows martial arts?

The Karate Squid.

■

How do you know when a bird is a criminal?

When it's a robin.

■

Why don't hens fight with other animals?

They're all chicken.

**What did the dog in the Old West
say when it limped into town?**

"I'm lookin' for the varmint who shot my paw."

■

**What do you call a
two-thousand-pound canary?**

Sir.

■

**What do you feed a
two-thousand-pound canary?**

Anything it wants.

■

**How do you get a
two-thousand-pound canary to sing?**

You ask it very, very nicely.

■

**If you dream that a wild rhinoceros
is charging at you, what time is it?**

Time to wake up.

■

**If you wake up and the rhinoceros
is right there in bed next to you,
what time is it?**

Time to get out of bed!

What did the male sheep say to the female sheep?

"I'm very fond of ewe."

■

What did the ewe say to the lamb when they went traveling?

"Fasten your sheep belt."

■

What did one cockroach say to the other?

"You bug me!"

■

What did the African explorer say when he got to the jungle?

"Safari, so goody."

■

What did the fast tomato say to the slow tomato?

"Ketchup!"

What did the male ape say to the female ape?

"You're the gorilla my dreams."

What did the big battery say to the other batteries?

"Charge!"

■

What did one house say to the other house?

"Honey, I'm home!"

■

What did one computer say to the other computer?

"Let's get digital."

■

What did the other computer say?

"First let's go get a byte."

■

What did one corpse say to the other?

"Quiet! Stop coffin!"

Why don't elephants fly?

They're afraid of heights.

■

Why don't elephants swim?

They don't like getting water in their ears.

■

What's the difference between an elephant and a plum?

Their color.

■

What did Tarzan say when he saw the elephants coming over the hill?

"Here come the elephants."

■

What did Jane say when she saw the elephants coming over the hill?

"Here come the plums." She was color-blind.

■

What do you get when you cross an elephant with a rhino?

Elefino.

How do you get down off an elephant?

You don't. You get down off a duck.

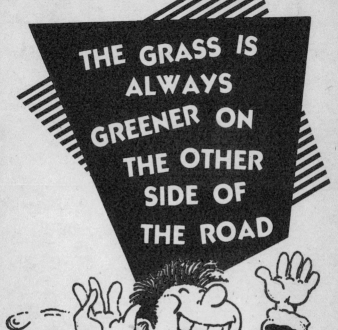

THE GRASS IS
ALWAYS
GREENER ON
THE OTHER
SIDE OF
THE ROAD

Why did the chicken cross the road?

To get to the other side.

◾

Why did the rooster cross the road?

To be with the chicken!

Why did the turtle cross the road?

To get to the shell station.

Why didn't the skeleton cross the road?

Because he didn't have the guts.

■

JIM: Why did the turkey cross the road?
KIM: To get *Time* magazine.
JIM: I don't get it.
KIM: Neither do I. I get *Newsweek*.

OH, THOSE WACKY EXTRA—TERRESTRIALS!

Why did the E.T. scientist move his clock forward?

He wanted to be ahead of his time.

■

Why did the E.T. take cream and sugar to the movies?

He heard they were going to have a serial.

■

Why did the E.T. take a ladder to the restaurant?

He heard that the french fries were on the house.

■

Why did the E.T. bring a picnic into the public garage?

He saw a sign saying PARK HERE.

■

Why did the E.T. walk all the way around town before cooking Chinese food?

He heard that you have to make Chinese food with a big wok (walk).

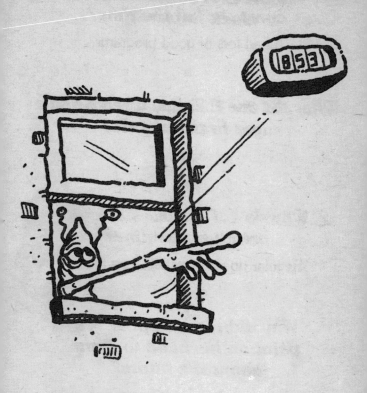

Why did the E.T. throw his atomic-powered digital clock out the window?

He wanted to see time fly.

Why did the E.T. watch his computer all the time?

It had lots of good programs.

•

What did the E.T. say when he saw the Ferris wheel?

"Mom!"

•

Why do E.T.s always ask for premium gasoline?

Regular doesn't quench their thirst.

•

Why did the E.T. pour red paint on his hand to learn about the future?

He wanted to get his palm red.

RETURN OF THE ROLLICKING RIDDLES

What sound does a rubber plane make when it hits the ground?

Boeing-Boeing!

■

How do you fix a leaky roof?

Open-house surgery.

■

Why do they have a fence around the cemetery?

Because people are dying to get in!

■

What is Dracula's favorite kind of boat?

A blood vessel.

■

What is Dracula's favorite kind of beans?

Human beans.

■

Why did Dracula get thrown in jail?

He was caught robbing a blood bank.

Why did the ghost like to go disco dancing?

Because he was a boogie man.

Why can't you starve in the desert?

Because of all the sand which is (sandwiches) there.

■

What has four wheels and flies?

A garbage truck.

■

Why is waiting by the phone a good way to get married?

Because sooner or later you're bound to get a ring.

■

What's the longest word in the world?

Smiles. There's a mile between the first and last letters.

■

Why did the javelin thrower practice in the music store?

He wanted to break a record.

What does a caveman call his cave?

Home sweet stone.

■

Where can you find extra belly buttons?

At the Navel Reserve.

■

What's black and white and black and white and black and white?

A penguin rolling down a hill.

■

What's red and white and red and white and red and white?

Santa Claus falling down a chimney.

■

What's red and green and red and green and red and green?

A frog in a blender.

■

What's green and has wheels?

Grass. (We lied about the wheels.)

If a train leaves New York for San Francisco at sixty miles an hour, and at the same time another train leaves San Francisco for New York at forty miles an hour, where will they meet?

Nowhere. East is east, and west is west, and never the train shall meet!

THERE'S NO TUNE LIKE A CARTOON!

HI, I'M A WIDE-MOUTHED FROG AND I EAT FLIES. WHO ARE YOU?
I'M AN ALLIGATOR AND I EAT WIDE-MOUTH FROGS.
OH, REALLY?